MAGA MY ASS

An Opinion Essay

Thoughts and Poetry

By
Johnny Spalione

MAGA MY ASS
An Opinion Essay
Thoughts and Poetry

For permissions or inquiries, contact:
Info@johnnyspalione.com

ISBN- 978-1-965408-84-1

Published and Printed by
Book Writing League
www.bookwritingleague.com

Dedication

This compilation of my opinion essay, subject poems and daily thoughts are a message to the soul of a nation that has thrived in Democracy and inspires to maintain touch with the root of that very dream that all men are created equal and brotherly love is a reason to look each other in the eye and hold each other in self-esteem that is mutually respected and accepted. It is dedicated to those that have not been swayed by the contemptuous deceit and blatant attack on the sovereignty of this country.

Acknowledgment

To the silent majority that has stepped up to battle this threat to Democracy and inner peace for the hard-working minority that makes up the majority of America.

Table of Contents

DADDY'S FOOTSTEP

By Johnny Spalione

You've been faithfully walking in Daddy's righteous footsteps.
Aimlessly blinded by obscured shadows of doubt.
Eagerly trying to be the man you were destined to be.
Until you woke up the world and the world figured it out.
That the corrupt and dirty path of those heavy footsteps.
Are deeply embroiled in the terrible wrongs of the past.
Those everyday dealings seemed so innocent then.
But the widespread hurt and the shameful pain ever lasts.

There's a new generation of dreamers who.
Gave victims strength to stand up and be heard.
And hope for the best of reasons to live.
And believe in their hearts that we trust in their words.
We don't condone indiscretion of money for lust.
Aren't afraid anymore to stand up and say no.
The power taken from the moral majority.
That accepts the sins of the wealthy for show.

Do as I say, not as I do.
Do it my way and I will give it to you.
The Good old Boy creed is to honor thy greed.
The Good old Boys are a dying breed.

In A Perfect World

In a perfect world...you'd be Adam and I'd be Eve.
Children of the earth with one God to believe in.
We'd be captured by the magic and live for the thrill.
To flourish in the beauty of nature's good will.
I'd tempt you with the apple and you'd tell me no lies.
We'd be bound to see life through innocent eyes.
We'd have the future to fear and the unknown to explore.
There'd be no state and no church, no threat of nuclear war.

In a perfect world...there's nothing money can buy.
We'd trade our trust and our respect for an honest smile.
There'd be no cancer, no aids, no envy and greed.
We won't go hungry or feel the threat of poverty.
There'd be an endless source of gold at the rainbow's end.
No price to pay for freedom or righteousness to defend.
There'd be peace on earth with no hostility.
No needless suffering or pointless pain and no humility.

In a perfect world...our demons would die and heroes come alive.
No alien invasion to encounter or red tape to despise.
There'd be no judgment or guilt for fools to deny.
No competition or injustice for victims to decry.
Time would stand still for the impatient soul.
There'd be no failure to flee, no unfulfilled goals.
We'd have no one's shoes to walk in but our own.
And no one's life to ridicule, no tyrant to overthrow.

Ponderance

by
Johnny Spalione
7-15-24

When I look up into the star filled sky,

My questions of what when and why,

Lead me to ask over and over again.

Why am I here and when will it end?

My journey through life here on earth.

Is it something to value with worth?

Am I witness to inevitable truths?

That have spiraled into chaos since youth.

The exponential growth of universal woes.

Continues the quest to define what we know.

As man explores the outer limits of space.

Hidden secrets expose the worldwide race.

To conquer questions of human existence.

And ponder the meaning of man's insistence.

On hiding the past to cover up the proof.

Of alien presence lost in the spoof.

THE SWAMP EXPLAINED

By
Johnny Spalione
7/13/24

People from all walks of life commence to,

Opining and whining for one side of the fence.

Living and dying for what they believe.

Intent on swaying the innocent deceived.

Total disregard for morals and truths untold.

Immature, conniving and disrespectfully bold.

Completely blinded by egotistical goals.

Ignorance blissfully taking control.

Absolute denial of the facts we see and are told.

Notwithstanding the fears as the story unfolds.

Sincerely devoted to complicit donor trolls...the swamp thrives.

YOU CAN'T UNSTIR THE MELTING POT

by Johnny Spalione

You can't unstir the melting pot.
You made the stew, that's what you got.
The trouble will brew when the tension is hot.
But You can't unstir the melting pot.

You tell me there's a divided America.
a polarization of the masses.
You warned me about the power of greed.
That drives social separation of the classes.
You tell me there's a divided America.
A disagreement played out in the public vain.
Each side ignores truth with indignant resignation.
To the facts about who's right and what's wrong once again.

You can't unstir the melting pot.
You made the stew, that's what you got.
The trouble will brew when the tension is hot.
But You can't unstir the melting pot.

You tell me there's a divided America.

You tell me there is a divided AAAmerikkka.
it simple to see the ones who wanted it all.
until finally others did right and answered the call.

there's only one way to fix those pots.
keeping adding more immigrants.
stir it up with their kid's kids.
the resulting brew making them.
the haves instead of the have nots.

Mike

You have stated some obvious points in plain block and white.

Problem is there are too many interpretations when you read between the lines. Depending on which side of the fence you're sitting.

We grew up with those trying to break down those fences, those barriers that define the fine line that the good old boys established.

You talk about capitalism. In principle it is what makes America great. In reality it's what keeps the fight for equality alive. Money is the root of all evil.

Lack of money makes people desperate. Desperation brings out the fight in the dog and the dog just wants to bite the owner. It's a vicious circle. We aspire to make enough money to retire comfortably but the battle to keep up with the Joneses and make sure our kids have all the same things other kids have just eats up the money faster than we make it. Saving is a challenge for most. Impossible for the majority because the budget is strained in the first place.

I'm pretty sure the 10 cent cup of coffee I bought 40 years ago is the same as the 3 dollar cup I drank today. Our kids are getting priced out of life.

Inflation is the way capitalism gets even with cost of living raises that keep the 24% profit margin steady. That is a vicious cycle!!

Melting Pot Becomes The Victim When The Dividing Line In Politics Is Drawn.

Friends can't talk to friends for fear that truths will end long time relationships. Each side, each view, each belief is skewed by the voice they are listening to. Conservatives will hand for twisted spins in their perception of reality when Fox News pundits have a mouthful of the Good Old Boys cock as they spurt out the irony that is their disbelief. The American Dream stops at their Not In My Backyard doorstep where the enormous exponential growth in capitalism is exploding in their faces as entrepreneurial youth have mastered the internet and joined enforce the 10 percenters.

Liberals sink with their steadfast dream of equality and freedom for all. Freedom acquired with financial independence and self-respect. But the fight for the almighty dollar is spread thin. Inflation and the cost of living perception is lost in the truth that the rich get richer no matter what. To grow profits beyond belief is not only super greedy but unreasonable to say the least. Struggling youth will rely on inheritance or trickle down luck.

3/25/23

The Good Old Boys have been making and breaking the rules as long as the masses were in the dark and ignorance was an excuse to be a loyal follower. But their promises were empty and the exponential growth of progress and knowledge of the truth has caught up to them.

They pulled the strings of well planted puppets to control the mislead belief that the cost of living is truly related to inflation. Truth is the capitalism thrives on profit. Profit at any cost. They took a good percentage of the pie and got used to it. Problem is that they have diminished the pie to an extent that only their greedy share is a true measure of the post expectations. The wealth they share is a far cry from the percentage of its value.

3/29

MAGA My Ass, An Opinion Essay

by Johnny Spalione

1/29/2021

MAGA my ass!! They say they want to see yesterday's glory rise again. They say they want it to be like the good old days when everyone had the same straight and narrow visions of freedom, free enterprise and freedom of worship. Everyone saw the same finish line and rode the wave of expansion to the future where lies a multitude of ways to seek opportunity for wealth, comfort and happiness. Everyone appeared to worship the same God, just different points of view with the idea that God's wish is that all men love one another. But did they ever stop to think about what they are really asking for? Did they ever look themselves in the eye and ask what it is they really want or need? Aren't they happy to be part of the American story that encourages the dreamer to live his dream where it is ok to be different and have different views? It was ok when they did it over there, out of sight, out of mind where their circle was big enough to protect them from being joined. Those hardened people in the circle watched pockets of different creeds, nationalities, religious beliefs and sexual orientation close in and squeeze the circle, trying to erase the lines that create the circle, trying to create equality for one and all. Maga my ass!!

America is and has never stopped being great for all the progress made in bringing peace and freedom to the world with undying understanding that all men are created equal. Untold leader for freedom and democracy that has led the free world against the will of dictators and all other threats to freedom so that each man and woman could enjoy the pursuit of happiness. The forefront of a people's republic that allows one and all the opportunity to contribute and thrive in the American way. Live free and prosper. Liberty and justice for all. Dream big and be somebody.

We have overcome enormous domestic shortcomings since the abolition of slavery and the acceptance of suffragettism. We have staved off the threat of communism and Islam extremists. We've witnessed the march for equality that has only shed a glistening ray of light on a glimpse of hope that has finally come to surface for the injustice to the black community because Black Lives Matter.

 Equal opportunity for minorities (oh we have come a long way) and the poor white working class was a tough pill to swallow, but the good old boy's economists figured a way to control the cost-of-living escalation and maintain the profit margin for big business on a growing scale that doesn't compare. The rich get richer as the hardworking middle-class muddles away in survival mode, with dreams to chase and work to be done. Slavery in disguise. Economic injustice served with a slice of American pie.

Black Justice and Women's rights were tough enough for the good old boys to swallow, but the LGBT movement threw them for a loop. Champions of righteousness, these God Fearing … holy rolling citizens gung-ho for redemption that won't accept the exodus from the closet of close friends and relatives. That grew up ignoring the truth, believing that the homosexuality was disgusting sin and instilled fear in the gay community. They have watched the movement turn denial and fear into acceptance and pride. Worldwide celebration of love, just part of the vast growth in man's appreciation for man and woman's appreciation for woman.

Human dignity takes a back seat to greed with those privileged few that think they own all the toys and should be able to make and break the rules and laws as they please. or change the laws for their advantage as we have seen of late. For some time, they have swept the unwanted truth under the rug to hide the facts and distort the views of an unknowing and ever trusting public. So true, the good old boys are fighting hard to keep that aura of invincibility that allowed them to break all the laws behind the whispers. Too many people turned a blind eye for too long. Their time has been coming and a lot of truth is coming out of the woodworks.

So true, the good old boys and proud boys are fighting hard to undo all the progress that has been made by the masses that make up the true voice of America, to break down the barriers to equality that will bring peace and harmony to all men and women that passed the open arms of the Statue of Liberty or were born free to American parents. Those bitter old souls that won't recognize and let the immense expansion of the universe flow with eternal change and total acceptance of the unknowing future will fight to preserve the wealth and comforts of greed and ignorance and dwell in the past's misfortunes and refuse to accept all of God's creations as equal partners in man's quest on earth to thrive and be happy.

Technology and modern advancement of science and mathematics and the vast pursuit of unlimited dreams have catapulted the human race into what used to be considered science fiction and senseless imagination. With the knowledge that comes with progress is the awakening by the unknowing public to the hidden facts and atrocities that have been happening right under our eyes for years and years. Not only Governments but Bankers and Corporate Bigwigs of our treasured institutions hide the perilous truths in an effort to protect the masses from mass hysteria. It was easy before the masses had unlimited access to information through the internet and now the social media platform that can spread news and information, good or bad, true or false with the blink of an eye. It takes a lot of time and effort to untangle the lies and deceit only to discover that the damning misinformation is merely a smoke screen to cover up the untold efforts of greed and corruption that makes a piranha out of a crocodile. Clean the swamp…sure did. Now nobody dares enter the swamp. But curiosity will always lead a cat to explore and chase the dream, sometimes to the edge of death. Some to the brink of insanity.

It is hard for me to imagine how so-called patriots can be so narrow minded as to think that someone of unlike mind is radical and un-American and should be treated with hatred and disdain because they are on the other side of an imaginary line that has been drawn like a kid warning to separate the privileged from the hard working dreamer that threatens to steal their security and reveal the ugly truths that keep them in the darkness of ignorance. They can't see that their own leader is so self-absorbed and pretentious that he would throw his most ardent supporter under the bus in a second to promote his own credibility of lies and corrupted deceit. They have latched onto the ideals of a madman that refuses to accept defeat and admit his willing contribution to the extreme actions of a confused mob that believes his mistruths and blatant lies. A

11

mob that defines what white supremacy stands for and domestic terrorism is all about. They follow a man that has thrown tons of shit on the chalk board for everyone to sort out to create an illusion that what he speaks is the truth. But he believes the very deceitful lies that define him and those desperate followers that have forgotten that this Democracy is based on laws made for the people, by the people. All the people, where the majority rules.

The sad truth is, is that the good old boys' heyday where the white majority ruled by ideals that allowed money to buy happiness, freedom and decisions of jurisprudence are being exposed and suppressed. The resilience of diversity will build the everlasting trust in community needed because the inevitable reality of being the America, one country, indivisible with justice for all is still on the forefront of the people's pursuit of equal justice and opportunity for all.

The fear that embroils the very idea that this melting pot of haves and have nots, whites, browns, yellows and blacks, Jews, Catholics, Muslims and Christians that have blended into the multi-cultural work of art known as American society that lives and breathes for the foundation of Democracy that assures us freedom of speech, religious beliefs and unending pursuit of happiness is facing its demise.

The promise of our forefathers to recognize the need for growth and change provided a belief that following the wishes of the masses to accept the inherent will of the people, we the people, will press forward with fight and determination to maintain the grasp of free will and free spirit for all mankind and celebrate it with the right to vote. The right to choose without being subjected to ridicule or rejection. The right to be part of the majority without defiance in acceptance of our voice. We will no longer be poked in the eye by the blinding force of discrimination or pushed aside by the strong arm of a one-sided law being enforced by the prejudiced side of society to ensure the comforts of the wealthy and privileged few. Social and human injustice will be on the forefront of the fight for Democratic freedom. The obscured visions of far right and left will be faced with truth and vindication by the unwavering growth of generations of believers in truth, equality and righteousness that serves us all.

I believe that we can move forward as a country on the mend by looking forward and working toward being the example-setting nation that is strong and formidable in the world-wide quest to overcome hatred and tyranny. A country that is not divided by political will. We can't un-stir the melting pot. We can't undo the injustice in our past whether it be systemic racialism by confederates and white traditionalists or economic throttling by the rich and privileged. We can only look to the horizon for mutual appreciation for each other's positive contributions to society as we spiral into the space age with more than global concerns for the environment and future of the earth.

Thought for the Day

8/19/23

By Johnny Spalione

I am patiently sitting and anxiously waiting in dreaded anticipation.

I sit in fear of the illicit contempt in the writing on the wall.

Seriously fed up with all the debating and unwanted intimidation.

The needless call to arms heard whispered in the hall.

Are we bound to be witness to an uncivil war?

As the divide in the country is like nothing we've seen before.

The definition of corruption is twisted in the winds.

Of deceit and dissention among the good old boys and their evil twins.

The Deep state we fear is deeper than the divide it has commandeered.

Since the search for condemnation finds them looking in the mirror.

So many in the past stood not so innocently blinded on the political fence.

Leaning toward their campaign dollars disguising their claims to common sense.

Like sheep, the hypnotic spell of the misled congregation.

Has led us to the slaughter of democracy that was defined by our founding fathers.

If brothers and friends stood true to the bond built with mutual love.

And understanding that all men and women are created and shall be equal.

Then there will be no one that can stand above the law in indignation.

And draw a line to be crossed in determined resignation.

Of the facts and truth that we are truly one nation under God.

Let no man be king!

Thoughts by Johnny Spalione 12/24/23

I am thoroughly amused by the ignorance displayed by all the Chumpsters that deny the simple truth that Donald is a blistering Bully that thinks only of himself and his wish to be king. His blatant disregard and disrespect for the people of this country is disheartening. He will continue to fill the chalk board with lies and deceitful rhetoric to cover up the truth that is his blinded belief in himself. He has his game plan to turn the tables and dispel the truth that is so very plain to see. His followers only want to believe what he says because they refuse to delve into the facts and truths that are very plain to see. Witness this on any YouTube parody that has the host ask Maga devotees simple questions about political facts and Donald's blatant lies. They are embarrassed yet distinctly firm in their belief in him, even after the facts are spelled out. He claims that there is a witch hunt and all is political. I say if we find a witch, which we have, then hunt the bitch down and get rid of the stench that comes with it. Truth is, he is a brilliant thief in the night that has screwed over so many people that he honestly believes it is ok because it is truly the American way. He deflects to the misguided souls that think the Biden's are crooked. Truth is that all politicians of the old school are entrenched in the unwritten belief that there is a hidden theme to limit the growth of the people and keep them under the thumb of the good old boys on both sides of the fence.

Bigotry is a real thing. Hatred for the other side is a serious problem because a line has been drawn in the sand by the greedy hands of resentful old schoolers as many groups of faith and color are breaking down barriers and grasping for reparations and due justice for lost time. The disguise of equality in the deep south and midwestern states has been lost in the woodwork.

12/25/23

Lost in the woodwork of society's unwavering denial of the hatred that divides the soul and infiltrates the spirit of America. Hidden in the shadows of whispered ideals are the fears that have driven a stake into the heart of the nation. The idea that the right to freedom and pursuit of happiness is roiled in the inherited greed spurned competitive nature of capitalism whereby the masses get swallowed up by the percentages as the wealthy moves the scale in their favor at unforgiving rates. Opportunity becomes a burden. The realization that success is harbored in the fact that one must take advantage of another to achieve the dream of prosperity. The more people the bigger the reward. To provide for mutual love is the ultimate sacrifice for the laboring man.

12/26/23

It is so simple to spell out and see the profound insanity that is the fight for equality in life driven by the almighty dollar. In a pie chart scenario, the slice of pie in the corporate world is bigger than the whole pie of the middle class. Even if you take equal proportions by percentage the difference is so overwhelming it is pitiful to think that the first reaction of the corporations is to raise the cost of living to recuperate the profit margin. This only puts the middle class back where they started…spending every last penny earned and building up credit debt to make ends meet.

12/27/23

The Rich get Richer for a reason. It goes back a long way into the depths of this economic disaster that is capitalism. Those with money not only funded and paid for life to happen, they created ways to make money from their money. They'd loan with interest due to those with dreams to have what the haves have. Over time the escalation of the population has created exponential growth of wealth to the wealthy as the demand for goods and competitiveness increases with power of the dollar. Inflation became a term to explain the need for greed as it limits the earning power of the working class.

12-29-2023

Lie and Deny…Lie and Deny.

When a liar is blowing smoke enough for his own blood to choke on the lies we despise.

A liar builds a fire to stoke and blinds us as he goes for broke on the lies we despise.

Refute and Dispute.

Refute and Dispute.

Unrehearsed, he speaks off the cuff, spouting racist nonsense and stuff.

Believing his guff and devotees won't call his bluff.

He fills up the chalk board with all kinds of thoughts and ideas…lies and mistruths.

True or False doesn't matter. It's a distorted misinterpreted thought.

A fascist narcissistic idea so misleading and deceiving.

When called on the lies. Defense turns to offensive bullying.

Refute ..dispute .. deter and deflect.

Bullyish calling out opponent as worse… the demon left. sees his self as a savior.

12-30-2023

Open your eyes, or listen to the music. He's singing the same old song.

The deeper we go he has darkened the verse. His demented point of view is a curse.

12-31-2023

Even though his ardent followers see his flaws and blatant misgivings, they still want to believe in him. They can't see that the truth before them is so simple to see and it is agreed upon. But the unwarranted acceptance of the lies and distorted vision of his distinct desire to be a dictator as a blessing to the protection of democracy is desperately lost in the whispering winds of his bullying ways. People think he is leading. People think his concept is strength. Buth the strength is a bundle of twisted rhetoric designed to keep everyone busy trying to figure out what is the end game? What is the root of his madness? We are figuring out or finally believing in mass the truth that is the Donald. An egotistical piece of shit that would throw anyone and everyone under the bus to save his own ass or better the Trump brand.

1-5-2024

From his devoted lawyer, Cohen, to many misguided GOP stalwarts that are turning over and uncovering the facts of Donald's belligerent insistence that is Democracy's savior, to finally see the light and know he is the biggest enemy in the fight.

Donald and family made a hundred times more tainted money than the Bidens or any other significant political leader, in the tumultuous discovery of the dark secret that is political support. Bribery was disguised as campaign funding.

It is astonishing to think that the political climate stirred up in the country has taken a turn for the worse. It seems that the Maga idiots have buckled down to try and wrest the country from Democracy and thrust it into the dreams of a madman hell bent on becoming the most powerful man in the world because he believes he is God's chosen savior. He thrives on misinformation and misleading his followers to believe he is working for the common man that makes up the working class when in fact he only sees the benefit for the 3%ers he thinks is doing the country justice in their shared visions of capitalism. He in fact was leading the charge in corrupt business practices that his followers perceive as brilliance when indeed it is pure dishonesty. His overwhelming love for Putin and Hitler is blinding his base and substantiating his cries for power to thwart the facts and truths that have defined America. Trickle down didn't materialize the way Reaganomics visionaries portrayed the economic travesty that has driven us into billionaire bliss that is lost in the greedy pursuit of control. Trickle down my ass! Those Reagan followers that probably had a truly genuine goal to help the middle class and downtrodden help themselves weren't smart enough or sharp enough to see that old dogs have all the tricks and will go to extreme depths to keep everything they have. They were oblivious to the obvious; the rich get richer for a reason. They keep peddling the lies created to deflect and protect the ugly truth that is their refusal to share the wealth.

Greed and corruption are killing the American dream. Loophole writers for corporate America have found ways to make equality a joke. They compare with percentages. The problem is that 10% of billions does not compare to 10% of thousands. Especially when the hit would come out of record profit earnings each year.

After the deregulation and overhaul of corporate America and big business buy out of mom and pop and other dreamers, Big business and big pharma have distorted the dream. There are too many Peters and too many Pauls.

Donald has sucked their dicks for so long he feels they owe a debt of gratitude and confirmation of his undying devotion to the almighty dollar.

I read blogs and commentary from far right Fox and see the anguish and fear boiling up in the masses as the lies and deception are distorted in the worst of ways. There are people in this country that think it is best to fight the idea that equality is an earned right and that confederacy is a long-lost tradition that harbors bigotry and hatred to the nth degree and they want it back!

I am disgusted with the idea that I have friends and colleagues that ignore the truth and fall for the false rhetoric and lies that are designed to quell the distrust in the piranha that has overtaken the swamp. Just like the lazy loyalists that won't look for the truth to satisfy their beliefs because it is easier to ignore the truth than it is to accept and try to change it. They know his lips are moving and they know what that is all about. His smug face is hiding the fear that every narcissist feels threatened by. Losing the hordes of misled sheep that are fattening his wallet and backing up the belief that he should be king.

2-10-2024

I wake up each morning with the intent on meditating and getting my day off to a good start. I go into the family room with my headphones and sit on the couch and wait for the cat to race up to the sliding glass door in anticipation of being let out. Most days I tune into YouTube and get in 30 minutes of powerful meditation music that is advertised to heal and enlighten you with universal secrets of the laws of abundance and attraction. An awakening of the third eye. Peaceful and serene.

Some days I get distracted and open up the Meidas Touch Network that has podcasters delving into the political nightmare surrounding Donald Trump and the Maga extremists. This channel with experts in law and government tries to view and report the facts as they see them and unravel the twisted extreme propaganda spewed by Fox and far right networks. They offer factual news that is either distorted or ignored by the maga republicans. Of late they have had defectors of the maga right on the show explaining and substantiating the lies that are being spread and defended by Donald and his followers. They have seen the light and want others to open their eyes and fall out of the hypnotic spell of the demonic dictator that is the Donald. They have denounced the Republican Party's obsession with him. The far right Christians that have confused what the freedom of religion aspect of the constitution is all about are trying to force their will and determination on the freedoms of speech and religion in the Good Old Boy fashion of my way or the highway. Even though they are fraught with dishonest leaders that twist their works enough to confuse and deceive them all.

The smugness that is smothered by his charm and charisma is a liar's main avenue to deceit and confusion that becomes the coverup to his madness. He conveniently forgets or has problems with the question when he can't tell the truth that sheds light on his corrupt ways and evil mind. The media says he is having cognitive issues. I say he is merely showing Pinocchio syndrome because he cannot tell the truth for fear that it will damage his reputation in broad daylight. His denial of the events that are shedding light on his corrupt ways is evident. The idea that he and his family are spending millions of his donor's dollars on their lawyers and personal battles in court is preposterous. He can't himself because he is the all-time crook.

It amuses me when he puts on his tough guy act and silently eggs his proud boy idealists to deal with protestors and opposers. The true bully that he is starting to show up more and more as his kingdom dwindles.

His ardent followers are figuring things out. Or confessing to the facts that they truly are bigots and fools that won't accept diversity and progression and want to fight to get those lost atrocities back. They ignore the proof and the blatant truth that he is a corrupt, dishonest narcissist that tells people what they want to hear. And since they only listen to him believe all he says is gospel. He is a master of deflection, confusion and false reassurance. He made up Fake News. Journalists have taken advantage of the chase for truth and decency. Trump with his chalkboard offense throws enough non existing issues for the press to chase and enough confusion for his base to be convinced that the other side is lying and they are the culprits in the grand scheme. He paints a rosy picture of the lies for his loyal 1% base to affirm his assurance to their greedy control of economics and

3-16-2024

I have been stifled by my emotions and disgust about the political climate that has dug its heels into the throat of America so much that I would not sit down to write. I instead spend my time with millions of people staring into my phone with deep intent, scrolling through the hilarious shorts on YouTube. I stumbled on to the Meidas Touch Network comprised of legal experts that try to point out the obvious truths that have been distorted and dispelled by the Maga idiots. It is dumbfounding and unbelievable to witness the narrow mindedness that has taken control of some of these people. Devout Trumpsters that are proud to stand by their man after admitting he is a crook and corrupt narcissist hell bent on becoming a King. They take his bullying style and smug banter as staunch leadership. They are closer and closer to admitting that MAGA is truly MAWA. Make America White Again! They believe his lies and stand by his failure to concede a loss. He is the sorest loser this planet has ever seen. A rich kid that never grew up and learned how to be responsible. An actor that can captivate a crowd with his devious charm. He has taken hard earned money from his PAC to pay his legal fees. A billionaire that needs money. How absurd. The root of his evil has come to light. His four year set up ended and he couldn't complete his takeover of the country. He got the Supreme court under his thumb and stole the Republican Party to keep the upper hand. Some of the old guard republicans are stepping up and denying his grip and recognizing the grift of his ways. He is the only president to make hundreds of millions of dollars while in office. Not to mention the money his family made. They were part of the Russian invasion of our voting system and vicious attempt to frame the Bidens with lies and lies about untrue crimes. He has convinced his base with baseless information and dirty little lies that Joe is the criminal and that the Justice system is part of the problem that needs to be absolved. Truth be known; it is the republican judges that have been found to be the crooked fraudulent thieves in the night. They are standing up for their man and it is scary. All the judges in the cases are delaying and doing their best to have their day in court after the elections so in the event Donald wins all the cases will be dropped. And we will be the ones in jail.

3-22-2024

So we are waking up to the reality that the Donald is broke. Can't come up with the bond money to challenge his lawsuits and debts and get his trials to the Supreme court where he can get his way. The charade that was his wealth is fading in the sunset.

And then it changes. Shocking as it seems. He goes public with his Truth Social site and stands to make a billion dollars. And he is selling Bibles. Teamed up with country star, Lee Greenwood, his bible includes copies of the declaration of independence and constitution etc. Ironic as hell. He is begging his followers for money as he boasts that he doesn't need it. It is truly depressing to fathom that the maga majority is generally stupid as hell. To believe in someone that is facing time in prison in multiple states. Someone that continues to lie and deny. He is a grifter and a thief. A con artist supreme. His base falls for his charades because they are pitifully dumb and refuse to listen to the facts. They believe his trash that his opposers are the root of all evil. They are the deep state. The fake news. Hell Donald created fake news! They don't believe that Russia is responsible for the lies that threw the Bidens under the bus and look the other way as Raskin and Moskowitz mock their ignorance and shred the non-evidence that is the ridiculous basis for impeachment of the President.

3-31-2024

America has a Dream

America is on the brink of defeat and despair.

Dazed and confused and desperation everywhere.

Corruption exploding in the highest courts.

The Grand Ole Party is sinking and out of sorts.

Democratic dreams are fading in the past.

As Maga extremists are pushing hard to end them fast.

A devious White Greed has overtaken the American dream.

As the fear of integration has strengthened their hateful theme.

They have squeezed the middle class to the bottom of the heap.

Where the fight for independence is all they can keep.

America is facing an inevitable doom.

As the right wing Christians try to claim all the room.

As they push their Church to the front of the State.

And destroy the constitution with a twist of fate.

But it is true blue Americans that can bring us hope from despair.

If we stand up and fight for their freedom to care.

If I reach out for the answers and face impending ridicule.

For seeking a way to unravel the false narratives on both sides of the fence.

I am merely delving deep into the mystery of the deception.

Trying to ease my ill at ease and the discomfort I sense.

2-21-25

I didn't pay attention to politics when I was an adolescent blossoming into a young teen. At least not enough to really know what was really going on. Not beyond deciphering the facts that helped me answer questions on the Civics and Social Studies tests in my junior high classes. I just knew from a poor boys perspective as "the rich own the playground and all the toys and if you were lucky you could get a job to make them richer and allow you to squeak by, then you are hovering at the middle of the middle class. I wasn't exposed to the closed door discussions among community decision makers.

Calling the Spirit of Democracy

The frustration grows with the grains of desperation as the future unfolds in slow motion. The crumbling of sanity is washed away with the raining of the tears and confused emotions that get trampled by the fear and distorted by the nonsense that is hurled into the wind like the gospel truth. But sprouting through the woodwork like lightning flickering through the cracks in a weathered wall is hope tethered to the dreamers' delusion and spirit that propels them to call.

Calling all free spirits and believers in Democracy.

Calling all everyday man that stands tall and works hard.

Calling all Americans trying to live the dream to speak up and speak out…stop the travesty!

Thought 5-8-25

The irony of Maga's undying commitment to believing the Orange Turd's word is lost in the translation from his lips to their ears mainly because he has convinced them with utter nonsense and complete lies. The lies he pretends to come true if told time and again. That is the Art!

His commitment to derail democracy and become King is blatantly displayed as he appoints criminals and puppets that are so far up his ass they are tripping over his bullshit live and up front. You'd think he has dirt on everyone in the world with his smug, privileged attitude.

Credit some Republicans in Congress that recognize the extreme ends that Maga will go.

Truth is coming to the forefront…Make America Great Again is all about White Supremacy. Rich White Supremacy. The need for control and domination. Corporate greed is trying to squash the small business and working class. Donald says the kids don't need mor dolls. I say the Rich don't need multiple houses, planes and such!

Certainly don't need taxpayers to pay for a 90 million dollar Birthday parade. A Nazi parade at that!

World leaders shrug their shoulders and roll their eyes at the ludicrous things that comes out of his mouth. He is so non presidential and his smug attitude is embarrassing.

Canada and Greenland stand up proudly to declare they are not for sale yet he responds like a spoiled brat hoping to see his mommy cave to his cuteness.

There is a bold difference between an extra doll and a bigger yacht. Between thousands of jobs for honest hard working Americans and unneeded cutbacks for very necessary work to pay for newly formed DOGE hypocrisy. The Rich get richer by letting others pay for them on the way up. Saving at the expense of less fortunate that flounders in the struggle to survive. The privileged few and those near the top of the 5% club thrive with a knife in their hands, ready to stab all of us in the back.

It is funny that some rich buffoon who has never experienced the pains of living paycheck to paycheck tries to tell those masses to chill and sweat it out.

Whiny Donald has to endure his demented embarrassment in Air Force One and his minions are devastated as they try to calm the torrent waters in the wake of this corrupt and deceitful plan to take a 400 million dollar grift so clearly planned out and not so cleverly disguised. The crooks walk a crooked line to the end.

Meanwhile friends are distancing themselves from friends to avoid the conflict that Donald initiates because the impact of the mess he has put the country in with the blatant corruption by Republican and Democratic control is ignored while he tries to be king.

www.ingramcontent.com/pod-product-compliance
Lightning Source LLC
Chambersburg PA
CBHW052026030426
42335CB00026B/3302